Great Works Instructional Guides for Literature

Magic Tree House

A guide for the books by Mary Pope Osborne
Great Works Author: Melissa Callaghan

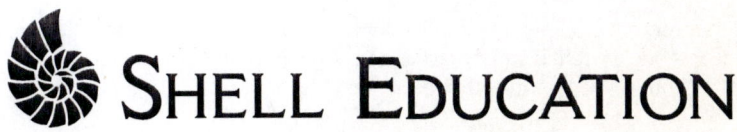

Publishing Credits

Corinne Burton, M.A.Ed., *President*; Emily R. Smith, M.A.Ed., *Content Director*; Lee Aucoin, *Multimedia Designer*; Kristy Stark, M.A.Ed., *Editor*; Stephanie Bernard, *Assistant Editor*; Don Tran, *Production Artist*

Image Credits

iStock (cover)

Standards

© 2007 Teachers of English to Speakers of Other Languages, Inc. (TESOL)
© 2007 Board of Regents of the University of Wisconsin System. World-Class Instructional Design and Assessment (WIDA)
© Copyright 2010. National Governors Association Center for Best Practices and Council of Chief State School Officers. All rights reserved.

Shell Education

a division of Teacher Created Materials
5301 Oceanus Drive
Huntington Beach, CA 92649-1030
ISBN 978-1-4807-8510-6
https://www.tcmpub.com/shell-education
© 2017 Shell Educational Publishing, Inc.

The classroom teacher may reproduce copies of materials in this book for classroom use only. The reproduction of any part for an entire school or school system is strictly prohibited. No part of this publication may be transmitted, stored, or recorded in any form without written permission from the publisher.

Table of Contents

How to Use This Literature Guide 4
    Theme Thoughts 4
    Vocabulary 5
    Analyzing the Literature 6
    Reader Response 6
    Guided Close Reading 6
    Making Connections 7
    Language Learning 7
    Story Elements 7
    Culminating Activity 8
    Comprehension Assessment 8
    Response to Literature 8

Correlation to the Standards 8
    Purpose and Intent of Standards 8
    How to Find Standards Correlations 8
    Standards Correlation Chart 9
    TESOL and WIDA Standards 10

About the Author—Mary Pope Osborne 11
    Possible Texts for Text Comparisons 11

Teacher Plans and Student Pages 12
    Pre-Reading Theme Thoughts 12
    Section 1: *Dinosaurs Before Dark* 13
    Section 2: *The Knight at Dawn* 23
    Section 3: *Mummies in the Morning* 33
    Section 4: *Pirates Past Noon* 43
    Section 5: The Magic Tree House Series 53
    Post-Reading Activities 62
    Post-Reading Theme Thoughts 62
    Culminating Activity: Compare and Contrast 63
    Culminating Activity: Climb the Steps! 64
    Comprehension Assessment 65
    Response to Literature: To the Rescue 67
    Response to Literature: The Magic Tree House Series 68
    Writing Paper 70

Answer Key 71

Introduction

How to Use This Literature Guide

Today's standards demand rigor and relevance in the reading of complex texts. The units in this series guide teachers in a rich and deep exploration of worthwhile works of literature for classroom study. The most rigorous instruction can also be interesting and engaging!

Many current strategies for effective literacy instruction have been incorporated into these instructional guides for literature. Throughout the units, text-dependent questions are used to determine comprehension of the book as well as student interpretation of the vocabulary words. The books chosen for the series are complex and are exemplars of carefully crafted works of literature. Close reading is used throughout the units to guide students toward revisiting the text and using textual evidence to respond to prompts orally and in writing. Students must analyze the story elements in multiple assignments for each section of the book. All of these strategies work together to rigorously guide students through their study of literature.

The next few pages describe how to use this guide for a purposeful and meaningful literature study. Each section of this guide is set up in the same way to make it easier for you to implement the instruction in your classroom.

Theme Thoughts

The great works of literature used throughout this series have important themes that have been relevant to people for many years. Many of the themes will be discussed during the various sections of this instructional guide. However, it would also benefit students to have independent time to think about the key themes of the books in the series.

Before students begin reading, have them complete the *Pre-Reading Theme Thoughts* (page 12). This graphic organizer will allow students to think about the themes of this series outside the context of the stories. They'll have the opportunity to evaluate statements based on important themes and defend their opinions. Be sure to keep students' papers for comparison to the *Post-Reading Theme Thoughts* (page 62). This graphic organizer is similar to the pre-reading activity. However, this time, students will be answering the questions from the point of view of Jack or Annie. They have to think about how the character would feel about each statement and defend their thoughts. To conclude the activity, have students compare what they thought about the themes before reading to what the characters discovered.

Introduction

How to Use This Literature Guide (cont.)

Vocabulary

Each teacher reference vocabulary overview page has definitions and sentences about how key vocabulary words are used in the specific book. These words should be introduced and discussed with students. Students will use these words in different activities throughout the book.

On some of the vocabulary student pages, students are asked to answer text-related questions about vocabulary words. The following question stems will help you create your own vocabulary questions if you'd like to extend the discussion.

- How does this word describe _____'s character?
- How does this word connect to the problem in this story?
- How does this word help you understand the setting?
- Tell me how this word connects to the main idea of this story.
- What visual pictures does this word bring to your mind?
- Why do you think the author used this word?

At times, you may find that more work with the words will help students understand their meanings and importance. These quick vocabulary activities are a good way to further study the words.

- Students can play vocabulary concentration. Make one set of cards that has the words on them and another set with the definitions. Then, have students lay them out on the table and play concentration. The goal of the game is to match vocabulary words with their definitions. For early readers or English language learners, the two sets of cards could be the words and pictures of the words.
- Students can create word journal entries about the words. Students choose words they think are important and then describe why they think each word is important within the book. Early readers or English language learners could instead draw pictures about the words in a journal.
- Students can create puppets and use them to act out the vocabulary words from the stories. Students may also enjoy telling their own character-driven stories using vocabulary words from the original stories.

Introduction

How to Use This Literature Guide (cont.)

Analyzing the Literature

After you have read each book with students, hold a small-group or whole-class discussion. Provided on the teacher reference pages for are leveled questions. The questions are written at two levels of complexity to allow you to decide which questions best meet the needs of your students. The Level 1 questions are typically less abstract than the Level 2 questions. These questions are focused on the various story elements, such as character, setting, and plot. Be sure to add further questions as your students discuss what they've read. For each question, a few key points are provided for your reference as you discuss the book with students.

Reader Response

In today's classrooms, there are often great readers who are below average writers. So much time and energy is spent in classrooms getting students to read on grade level that little time is left to focus on writing skills. To help teachers include more writing in their daily literacy instruction, each section of this guide has a literature-based reader response prompt. Each of the three genres of writing is used in the reader responses within this guide: narrative, informative/explanatory, and opinion. Before students write, you may want to allow them time to draw pictures related to the topic.

Guided Close Reading

Within each section of this guide, it is suggested that you closely reread a portion of the text with your students. Page numbers are given, but since some versions of the books may have different page numbers, the sections to be reread are described by location as well. After rereading the section, there are a few text-dependent questions to be answered by students.

Working space has been provided to help students prepare for the group discussion. They should record their thoughts and ideas on the activity page and refer to it during your discussion. Rather than just taking notes, you may want to require students to write complete responses to the questions before discussing them with you.

Encourage students to read one question at a time and then go back to the text and discover the answer. Work with students to ensure that they use the text to determine their answers rather than making unsupported inferences. Suggested answers are provided in the answer key.

How to Use This Literature Guide (cont.)

Guided Close Reading (cont.)

The generic open-ended stems below can be used to write your own text-dependent questions if you would like to give students more practice.

- What words in the story support . . . ?
- What text helps you understand . . . ?
- Use the book to tell why _____ happens.
- Based on the events in the story, . . . ?
- Show me the part in the text that supports . . . .
- Use the text to tell why . . . .

Making Connections

The activities in this section help students make cross-curricular connections to mathematics, science, social studies, fine arts, or other curricular areas. These activities require higher-order thinking skills from students but also allow for creative thinking.

Language Learning

A special section has been set aside to connect the literature to language conventions. Through these activities, students will have opportunities to practice the conventions of standard English grammar, usage, capitalization, and punctuation.

Story Elements

It is important to spend time discussing what the common story elements are in literature. Understanding the characters, setting, plot, and theme can increase students' comprehension and appreciation of the story. If teachers begin discussing these elements in early childhood, students will more likely internalize the concepts and look for the elements in their independent reading. Another very important reason for focusing on the story elements is that students will be better writers if they think about how the stories they read are constructed.

In the story elements activities, students are asked to create work related to the characters, setting, or plot. Consider having students complete only one of these activities. If you give students a choice on this assignment, each student can decide to complete the activity that most appeals to him or her. Different intelligences are used so that the activities are diverse and interesting to all students.

Introduction

How to Use This Literature Guide (cont.)

Culminating Activity

At the end of this instructional guide is a creative culminating activity that allows students the opportunity to share what they've learned from reading the books in the series. This activity is open ended so that students can push themselves to create their own great works within your language arts classroom.

Comprehension Assessment

The questions in this section require students to think about the books they've read as well as the words that were used in the books. Some questions are tied to quotations from the books to engage students and require them to think about the text as they answer the questions.

Response to Literature

Finally, students are asked to respond to the literature by drawing pictures and writing about the characters and stories. A suggested rubric is provided for teacher reference.

Correlation to the Standards

Shell Education is committed to producing educational materials that are research and standards based. As part of this effort, we have correlated all of our products to the academic standards of all 50 states, the District of Columbia, the Department of Defense Dependents Schools, and all Canadian provinces.

Purpose and Intent of Standards

The Every Student Succeeds Act (ESSA) mandates that all states adopt challenging academic standards that help students meet the goal of college and career readiness. While many states already adopted academic standards prior to ESSA, the act continues to hold states accountable for detailed and comprehensive standards. Standards are statements that describe the criteria necessary for students to meet specific academic goals. They define the knowledge, skills, and content students should acquire at each level. State standards are used in the development of our products, so educators can be assured they meet state academic requirements.

How to Find Standards Correlations

To print a customized correlation report of this product for your state, visit our website at www.teachercreatedmaterials.com/administrators/correlations/ and follow the online directions. If you require assistance in printing correlation reports, please contact our Customer Service Department at 1-877-777-3450.

Correlation to the Standards (cont.)

Standards Correlation Chart

The lessons in this book were written to support today's college and career readiness standards. The following chart indicates which lessons address each standard.

College and Career Readiness Standards	Section
Read closely to determine what the text says explicitly and to make logical inferences from it; cite specific textual evidence when writing or speaking to support conclusions drawn from the text. (R.1)	Analyzing the Literature Sections 1–5; Guided Close Reading Sections 1–5; Making Connections Section 5; Story Elements 5; Post-Reading Activities
Analyze how and why individuals, events, or ideas develop and interact over the course of a text. (R.3)	Analyzing the Literature Sections 1–5; Story Elements Sections 1–5
Interpret words and phrases as they are used in a text, including determining technical, connotative, and figurative meanings, and analyze how specific word choices shape meaning or tone. (R.4)	Vocabulary Sections 1–5
Analyze the structure of texts, including how specific sentences, paragraphs, and larger portions of the text (e.g., a section, chapter, scene, or stanza) relate to each other and the whole. (R.5)	Language Learning Section 4
Analyze how two or more texts address similar themes or topics in order to build knowledge or to compare the approaches the authors take. (R.9)	Culminating Activity: Compare and Contrast
Read and comprehend complex literary and informational texts independently and proficiently. (R.10)	Entire Unit
Write arguments to support claims in an analysis of substantive topics or texts using valid reasoning and relevant and sufficient evidence. (W.1)	Reader Response Sections 2–3; Making Connections Section 5
Write informative/explanatory texts to examine and convey complex ideas and information clearly and accurately through the effective selection, organization, and analysis of content. (W.2)	Making Connections Section 4; Reader Response Section 4; Story Elements Section 1
Write narratives to develop real or imagined experiences or events using effective technique, well-chosen details and well-structured event sequences. (W.3)	Reader Response Sections 1, 5; Story Elements Sections 2–4; Language Learning Section 2
Produce clear and coherent writing in which the development, organization, and style are appropriate to task, purpose, and audience. (W.4)	Reader Response Sections 1–5; Story Elements Sections 1–4; Language Learning Sections 1, 3
Develop and strengthen writing as needed by planning, revising, editing, rewriting, or trying a new approach. (W.5)	Language Learning Section 5; Story Elements Section 1
Conduct short as well as more sustained projects based on focused questions, demonstrating understanding of the subject under investigation. (W.7)	Culminating Activities

Introduction

Standards Correlation Chart *(cont.)*

College and Career Readiness Standards	Section
Draw evidence from literary or informational texts to support analysis, reflection, and research. (W.9)	Reader Response Sections 2–3; Post-Reading Theme Thoughts
Demonstrate command of the conventions of standard English grammar and usage when writing or speaking. (L.1)	Language Learning Sections 1–5; Story Elements Section 1
Demonstrate command of the conventions of standard English capitalization, punctuation, and spelling when writing. (L.2)	Language Learning Section 5; Story Elements Section 1
Apply knowledge of language to understand how language functions in different contexts, to make effective choices for meaning or style, and to comprehend more fully when reading or listening. (L.3)	Guided Close Reading Sections 1–5; Language Learning Section 4
Determine or clarify the meaning of unknown and multiple-meaning words and phrases by using context clues, analyzing meaningful word parts, and consulting general and specialized reference materials, as appropriate. (L.4)	Vocabulary Sections 1–5
Demonstrate understanding of figurative language, word relationships, and nuances in word meanings. (L.5)	Language Learning Section 4
Acquire and use accurately a range of general academic and domain-specific words and phrases sufficient for reading, writing, speaking, and listening at the college and career readiness level; demonstrate independence in gathering vocabulary knowledge when encountering an unknown term important to comprehension or expression. (L.6)	Vocabulary Sections 1–5

TESOL and WIDA Standards

The lessons in this book promote English language development for English language learners. The following TESOL and WIDA English Language Development Standards are addressed through the activities in this book:

- **Standard 1:** English language learners communicate for social and instructional purposes within the school setting.

- **Standard 2:** English language learners communicate information, ideas and concepts necessary for academic success in the content area of language arts.

Introduction

About the Author—Mary Pope Osborne

Mary Pope Osborne was born on May 20, 1949, in Fort Sill, Oklahoma. While living as a young child in Salzburg, Austria, the castle across the street from her family's home fueled Osborne's imagination. She always used her imagination to pretend exciting things were happening. She later stretched her imagination by acting in the theater. Since she moved a lot as a child, she got to travel to many exciting places.

Osborne also uses her rich imagination to create lively adventures for Jack and Annie as they travel to exciting times and exciting places. The first book in the Magic Tree House series, *Dinosaurs Before Dark*, was published in 1992. Osborne has added to the scope of her writing by including research guides to go along with many of her books. She has written 54 Magic Tree House books to date. She also writes the Mysteries of Spider Kane series, young adult novels, picture books, biographies, and retellings of fairy tales and fables.

Osborne is a big supporter of schools, teachers, and students. She started the Mary Pope Osborne Classroom Adventures program, which donates books to classrooms in Title I schools.

Possible Texts for Text Comparisons

In the first 28 books of the Magic Tree House series, Osborne has Jack and Annie helping Morgan le Fay, the head librarian of Camelot. Beginning with book 29, the series title changes to the Magic Tree House: A Merlin Mission and each book features the brother and sister team going on missions assigned by Merlin the magician. Common to all the books is Jack and Annie's love of learning and adventure and their strong and supportive sibling relationship.

Introduction   Name _____   Date _____

Pre-Reading Theme Thoughts

Directions: Draw a picture of a happy face or a sad face. Your face should show how you feel about each statement. Then, use words to say what you think about each statement.

Statement	How Do You Feel? 😊 ☹️	Explain Your Answer
Real things are always better than make-believe.		
Reading about things is better than experiencing them in real life.		
It can be fun to hang out with your little brother or sister.		
Older brothers or sisters are always braver than their younger siblings.		

Section 1: Dinosaurs Before Dark

Book Summary of *Dinosaurs Before Dark*

In Frog Creek, Pennsylvania, Jack and his sister, Annie, find a magical tree house that transports them to different times and places. The tree house is filled with books that immediately capture Jack's interest in learning and Annie's love of adventure. In *Dinosaurs Before Dark*, Jack and Annie open a book about dinosaurs to a picture of a Pteranodon. Jack wishes that he could see a real Pteranodon, and that is exactly what happens! Jack and Annie happily walk among dinosaurs until they meet a hungry Tyrannosaurus rex. Annie asks the Pteranodon to save Jack so that they can make it safely back home.

Cross-Curricular Connection

Dinosaurs Before Dark can be used in conjunction with units on dinosaurs, family relationships, and geography.

Possible Texts for Text Sets

- Aliki. 1988. *Digging Up Dinosaurs*. HarperCollins.
- Aliki. 1986. *Dinosaurs Are Different*. HarperCollins.
- Bjork, Christina. 2012. *Linnea in Monet's Garden*. Sourcebooks Jabberwocky.
- Havill, Juanita. 1990. *Jamaica Tag-Along*. HMH Books for Young Readers.
- Polacco, Patricia. 2014. *Clara and Davie*. Scholastic Press.

Section 1
Dinosaurs Before Dark

Vocabulary Overview

Key words and phrases from this section are provided below with definitions and sentences about how the words are used in the story. Introduce and discuss these important vocabulary words with students. If you think these words or other words in the story warrant more time devoted to them, there are suggestions in the introduction for other vocabulary activities (page 5).

Word	Definition	Sentence about Text
pretend (ch. 1)	make-believe	Jack prefers real things over **pretend** things.
glanced (ch. 2)	gave a quick look	Jack **glances** at all the books.
gliding (ch. 2)	moving silently and effortlessly	The Pteranodon is **gliding** over the tree house.
whistling (ch. 2)	making a shrill sound	The wind is **whistling** in the trees.
absolutely (ch. 2)	completely	It is **absolutely** quiet.
stream (ch. 3)	a body of running water	The **stream** flows through the field.
ancient (ch. 3)	from a period of time long ago	The **ancient** Pteranodon lands near the tree house.
examine (ch. 4)	to look at or check carefully	Jack wants to **examine** the Pteranodon.
alert (ch. 4)	watchful and ready to meet danger	The Pteranodon has an **alert** gaze.
caption (ch. 5)	the description of a picture	The **caption** says the Pteranodon weighed over 12,000 pounds.
medallion (ch. 5)	a large medal	The **medallion** has the letter *M* on it.
panic (ch. 8)	to feel overwhelming fear	Jack tells himself not to **panic** when he sees the Tyrannosaurus rex.

Name _____ Date _____

Dinosaurs Before Dark

Vocabulary Activity

Directions: Draw lines to complete the sentences.

Beginnings of Sentences	Endings of Sentences
Jack read the **caption**	when he sees the Tyrannosaurus rex.
Jack likes real things, but	as the tree house begins to spin.
Jack could not believe	to learn more about the Pteranodon.
Jack tries not to **panic**	they were looking at **ancient** creatures.
The wind starts **whistling**	Annie likes **pretend** things.

Directions: Answer this question.

1. Why does Jack want to **examine** the Pteranodon?

_____

_____

Section 1
Dinosaurs Before Dark

Teacher Plans

Analyzing the Literature

Provided here are discussion questions you can use in small groups, with the whole class, or for written assignments. Each question is written at two levels so that you can choose the right question for each group of students. For each question, a few key points are provided for your reference as you discuss the book with students.

Story Element	Level 1	Level 2	Key Discussion Points
Character	What does Jack think about Annie?	What kind of relationship does Jack have with Annie?	Jack is sometimes frustrated with Annie because she loves pretend things and he prefers real things; however, he cares for her and helps keep her safe.
Character	What does Annie think about Jack?	What kind of relationship does Annie have with Jack?	Annie understands Jack's love of books and how he likes to see the world; however, she likes to experience things and not just read about them.
Plot	What happens when Jack wishes to see a Pteranodon?	How does the tree house get transported to the time of the dinosaurs?	When Jack wishes to see the Pteranodon, the tree house transports Jack and Annie to the time of the dinosaurs—64 million years ago.
Setting	What is the setting at the beginning of this book?	Compare and contrast the different settings of the book.	At the beginning, the setting is in the woods near the kids' house. Then, the setting changes to the time of the dinosaurs, 64 million years ago. The area is home to Triceratops, Pteranodon, Anatosaurus, and Tyrannosaurus rex.

Name _____ Date _____

Dinosaurs Before Dark

Reader Response

Think

Think about a day when you had to spend time with a younger brother, sister, friend, or cousin. How did you feel about spending time with them?

Narrative Writing Prompt

Write about a day when you had to spend time with someone younger. What did you do together? Were you patient or frustrated with them?

_____
_____
_____
_____
_____
_____
_____
_____
_____
_____
_____
_____

Dinosaurs Before Dark

Name _____ Date _____

Guided Close Reading

Closely reread the part in chapter 9 when Jack rides the Pteranodon.

Directions: Think about these questions. In the space below, write ideas or draw pictures as you think. Be ready to share your answers.

❶ What do you learn about Jack when he tells himself, "Don't think. Just do it!"?

❷ What words in this section describe how Jack feels about flying on the Pteranodon?

❸ What words from the text tell you that it is difficult for the Pteranodon to carry Jack?

Name _____ Date _____

Dinosaurs Before Dark

Making Connections–Travel through History

Directions: The tree house is filled with books about exciting times and places. If you could climb the ladder to the tree house, what titles would you hope to find? Draw four book covers. Be sure to include a title and a cover illustration for each.

Dinosaurs Before Dark

Name _____ Date _____

Language Learning-Contractions

Directions: Circle the contraction in each sentence. Then, write the two words that make up each contraction.

> ### Language Hints!
> A contraction is a combination of two words. When the words are combined, letters are left out. That is where the apostrophe goes.

1. "The (monster's) coming!" _monster_ _is_

2. "It's time to go home." _____ _____

3. "I've never seen it before." _____ _____

4. "But I'm going up." _____ _____

5. "There's our house." _____ _____

Name _____ Date _____

Dinosaurs Before Dark

Story Elements-Setting

Directions: Jack and Annie are transported from their home in Frog Creek, Pennsylvania, to the time of the dinosaurs. Think about the two settings. Describe five things that are different between them.

1. _____

2. _____

3. _____

4. _____

5. _____

Dinosaurs Before Dark

Name _____ Date _____

Story Elements–Plot

Directions: Annie suggests that they do not tell anyone about what happens in the tree house. Jack agrees, since he thinks no one will believe them, but he writes about their adventures in his notebook. Write an entry in his notebook telling the main events in the story in the order they happen.

Section 2
The Knight at Dawn

Book Summary of The Knight at Dawn

In Frog Creek, Pennsylvania, Jack and his sister, Annie, find a magical tree house that transports them to different times and places. The tree house is filled with books that immediately capture Jack's interest in learning and Annie's love of adventure.

In *The Knight at Dawn*, Jack and Annie are having trouble sleeping as they think about the tree house they found in the woods near their home. Even though it is not yet dawn, Annie convinces Jack to go back to the tree house. Annie makes a wish to see the knight from one of the books, and suddenly, Jack and Annie feel the tree house start to spin. Looking out the window, Jack sees a castle. He thinks they should go home and make a plan, but Annie charges ahead toward the castle. Jack has no choice but to follow her. They are captured, but Annie tricks the guards with her flashlight so they can escape. While escaping from the castle, they fall into the moat. The knight rescues them and takes them back to the tree house. Safely back home, Jack realizes he has a memento with the letter *M* on it—the bookmark from the castle book.

Cross-Curricular Connection

The Knight at Dawn can be used in conjunction with units on medieval history, celebrations around the world, and architecture.

Possible Texts for Text Sets

- Aliki. 1986. *A Medieval Feast*. HarperCollins.
- Coombs, Rachel. 2009. *A Year in a Castle*. First Avenue Editions.
- DePaola, Tomie. 1998. *The Knight and the Dragon*. Puffin.
- O'Brien, Patrick. 1998. *The Making of a Knight*. Charlesbridge.

Section 2
The Knight at Dawn

Vocabulary Overview

Key words and phrases from this section are provided below with definitions and sentences about how the words are used in the story. Introduce and discuss these important vocabulary words with students. If you think these words or other words in the story warrant more time devoted to them, there are suggestions in the introduction for other vocabulary activities (page 5).

Word	Definition	Sentence about Text
crept (ch. 1)	moved along slowly and quietly	Jack **creeps** down the stairs without making a sound.
dashed (ch. 1)	moved with sudden speed	Jack and Annie **dash** across the yard on the way to the tree house.
glared (ch. 1)	stared angrily	Jack **glared** at Annie when she tried to scare him.
shuddered (ch. 2)	trembled with fear	Jack **shudders** as he remembered the Tyrannosaurus rex.
neighing (ch. 2)	making the loud cry of a horse	Jack and Annie hear a horse **neighing** outside the tree house.
armor (ch. 2)	a cover to protect the body in battle	A knight in full **armor** sits on a horse.
moan (ch. 2)	to make a long, low sound	The wind begins to **moan** as the tree house spins.
tremble (ch. 2)	to shake	The wind makes the leaves **tremble**.
moat (ch. 3)	a deep trench around the walls of a castle	To cross the **moat**, the drawbridge must be lowered.
feast (ch. 3)	a meal with plenty of food and drink	Music is played to announce each new dish at the **feast**.
dungeon (ch. 6)	a dark prison, usually underground	The guards take Jack and Annie to the **dungeon**.
precipice (ch. 7)	a steep and high wall of a castle	The **precipice** of the castle is above the moat.

Name _____ Date _____

The Knight at Dawn

Vocabulary Activity

Directions: Choose at least two words from the story. Draw a picture that shows what these words mean. Label your picture.

Words from the Story

| armor | moat | precipice | feast | dungeon |

Directions: Answer this question.

1. What creature does Jack worry might be in the **moat** around the castle?

_____

Section 2
The Knight at Dawn

Analyzing the Literature

Provided here are discussion questions you can use in small groups, with the whole class, or for written assignments. Each question is written at two levels so that you can choose the right question for each group of students. For each question, a few key points are provided for your reference as you discuss the book with students.

Story Element	Level 1	Level 2	Key Discussion Points
Character	Where does Annie see the windmill?	How does Jack observe the windmill?	Annie sees the windmill through the mist near the castle. Jack sees a picture of the windmill in his book.
Character	Who brings a flashlight?	Describe what Jack and Annie each bring to the tree house.	Annie brings a flashlight. Jack brings his notebook and a pencil.
Plot	What does Jack bring back from their trip to the castle?	What is special about the items they bring back from their adventures?	Jack brings back a leather bookmark. The leather bookmark from the castle and the medallion both have the letter *M* on them.
Setting	Describe the two settings of the story.	How did the setting impact Annie's use of the flashlight as a magic wand?	The two settings are present-day Frog Creek, Pennsylvania, and a castle in medieval times. The setting in the castle is long before the invention of any mechanical lighting devices, making the science of the flashlight appear like magic.

Name _____ Date _____

The Knight at Dawn

Reader Response

Think

Think about a time when you got to do something new or different. What did you do to get ready?

Opinion Writing Prompt

Tell if you agree or disagree with the following statement: *Before you do anything new, you should always plan and prepare.*

_____
_____
_____
_____
_____
_____
_____
_____
_____
_____
_____
_____

The Knight at Dawn

Name _____ **Date** _____

Guided Close Reading

Closely reread chapter 3. Begin with Jack and Annie looking at the windmill, and read through the end of the chapter.

Directions: Think about these questions. In the space below, write ideas or draw pictures as you think. Be ready to share your answers.

❶ What in the text tells you how Annie likes to learn about new things?

❷ How does the conversation between Jack and Annie help you to learn more about these characters? Use examples from the text.

❸ How does the author describe the setting?

Name _____ Date _____

The Knight at Dawn

Making Connections–A Weighty Problem

Directions: Knights wore suits of armor and were covered in metal from head to toe. Jack reads that a knight's helmet could weigh as much as 40 pounds. Sketch a picture of a knight in armor. Use your picture to estimate what the entire suit of armor might weigh, including the 40 pounds for the helmet.

The Knight at Dawn

Name _____ Date _____

Language Learning–Writing a Friendly Letter

Directions: Pretend you are Jack. Write a letter to the owner of the tree house. Think about the questions you would like to ask about the tree house. In your letter, include anything else you would like to tell the owner.

Language Hints!

- Use a comma after your greeting.
- Use a comma after your closing.

_____

_____

_____

_____

_____

_____

_____

_____

                             _____

                             _____

Name _____ Date _____

The Knight at Dawn

Story Elements–Character

Directions: Jack likes to think about things before he acts. He always has a notebook and a pencil in his backpack. If he travels again in the tree house, what else should he take? Draw and label Jack's backpack with the things you think would be useful to him.

The Knight at Dawn

Name _____ Date _____

Story Elements–Plot

Directions: The guards capture Jack and Annie, but the two kids are able to escape. Write a conversation between the three guards as they try to figure out how Jack and Annie were able to escape.

Section 3
Mummies in the Morning

Book Summary of *Mummies in the Morning*

In Frog Creek, Pennsylvania, Jack and his sister, Annie, find a magical tree house that transports them to different times and places. The tree house is filled with books that immediately capture Jack's interest in learning and Annie's love of adventure.

As Jack and Annie return to the tree house, they find a book about ancient Egypt. Jack loves pyramids! Jack points to the picture of the pyramid and wishes to go there. The tree house takes Jack and Annie to ancient Egypt. They follow a black cat into a pyramid where they meet the ghost of an Egyptian queen. Jack and Annie help the queen find the Book of the Dead so she can move on to the next life.

Cross-Curricular Connection

Mummies in the Morning can be used in conjunction with units on ancient Egyptian history, architecture, archeology, and geometry.

Possible Texts for Text Sets

- Aliki. 1985. *Mummies Made in Egypt.* HarperCollins.
- Boyer, Crispin. 2012. *National Geographic Kids Everything Ancient Egypt: Dig Into a Treasure Trove of Facts, Photos, and Fun.* National Geographic Children's Books.
- Levy, Janey. 2005. *The Great Pyramid of Giza: Measuring Length, Area, Volume, and Angles (Math for the Real World).* Rosen Publishing Group.
- Milton, Joyce. 2000. *Hieroglyphs.* Grosset and Dunlap.

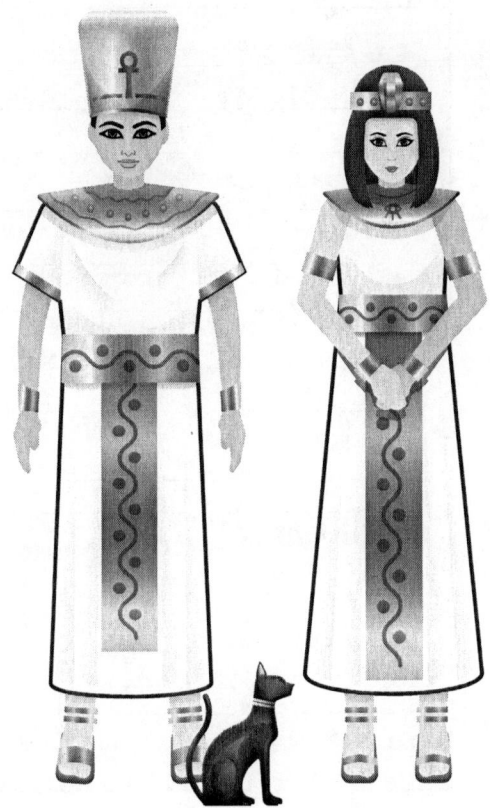

Section 3
Mummies in the Morning

Vocabulary Overview

Key words and phrases from this section are provided below with definitions and sentences about how the words are used in the story. Introduce and discuss these important vocabulary words with students. If you think these words or other words in the story warrant more time devoted to them, there are suggestions in the introduction for other vocabulary activities (page 5).

Word	Definition	Sentence about Text
pyramid (ch. 1)	a massive structure built in ancient Egypt to house the dead	Jack and Annie follow the cat into the **pyramid**.
sarcophagus (ch. 2)	a stone coffin	A mummy is placed in a **sarcophagus**.
mummy (ch. 2)	a body prepared for burial in the manner of the ancient Egyptians	Jack is excited to see the **mummy**, but Annie thinks it is gross.
mirage (ch. 2)	an illusion; something that seems to be real but is not actually there	Jack thinks the burial procession is a **mirage**.
torches (ch. 3)	long sticks that burn on one end and are carried by hand	Jack holds the book near the **torches** to read by the light.
tomb (ch. 4)	a burial chamber for dead people	**Tomb** robbers try to steal the scepter.
hieroglyphs (ch. 5)	characters used in ancient Egyptian writing	Jack describes the **hieroglyphs** to Queen Hupeti.
carved (ch. 6)	cut into a surface	The hieroglyphs are **carved** into the stone.
puzzled (ch. 6)	confused	The queen is **puzzled** by Jack's description of the symbol.
scroll (ch. 7)	a roll of paper that has been prepared as a writing surface	Jack places the **scroll** next to the mummy.
skull (ch. 8)	the structure of bone that forms the skeleton of the head	The bandages are falling off the mummy's **skull**.
budge (ch. 9)	to move slightly	No matter how hard they push, the door does not **budge**.

Name _____ Date _____

Mummies in the Morning

Vocabulary Activity

Directions: Practice your writing skills. Write at least two sentences using words from the story.

Words from the Story

pyramid	sarcophagus	mummy	mirage
tomb	carved	puzzled	scroll
budge	torches	skull	hieroglyphs

_____

_____

_____

_____

_____

_____

_____

Directions: Answer this question.

1. How does Jack help Queen Hutepi identify the last part of the **hieroglyphs**?

_____

_____

Section 3
Mummies in the Morning

Analyzing the Literature

Provided here are discussion questions you can use in small groups, with the whole class, or for written assignments. Each question is written at two levels so that you can choose the right question for each group of students. For each question, a few key points are provided for your reference as you discuss the book with students.

Story Element	Level 1	Level 2	Key Discussion Points
Plot	How does Annie feel about getting the Book of the Dead back to Queen Hutepi?	Why doesn't Annie place the Book of the Dead next to Queen Hutepi?	Annie feels that Queen Hutepi should not have to wait another moment to get back the Book of the Dead. Annie doesn't want to get close to the mummy because she thinks it's gross.
Character	What does Annie think of the mummy of Queen Hutepi?	Contrast how Jack and Annie react to the mummy of Queen Hutepi.	Annie thinks mummies are gross. Jack is very interested in the mummy and wants to examine it closely, while Annie has Jack place the book next to it so she won't have to get too close.
Setting	How do Jack and Annie escape the false passage in the pyramid?	What is the purpose of the false passages in the pyramid?	The black cat leads Jack and Annie out of the false passages. The false passages are meant to trap tomb robbers.
Plot	What does Annie find on the floor of the tree house?	What is the significance of what Annie discovers on the floor of the tree house?	Annie finds a glowing letter M on the floor of the tree house. This confirms that the tree house belongs to the mysterious M person.

Name _____ Date _____

Mummies in the Morning

Reader Response

Think

Think about how you act in new situations. Do you jump right into the situation, or do you take time to plan and think? Are you more like Annie or more like Jack in new situations?

Opinion Writing Prompt

When you face a new situation, would you rather be with Jack or Annie? Why?

_____
_____
_____
_____
_____
_____
_____
_____
_____
_____

Mummies in the Morning

Name _____ Date _____

Guided Close Reading

Closely reread the beginning of chapter 9 through the part when Jack and Annie escape the false passages.

Directions: Think about these questions. In the space below, write ideas or draw pictures as you think. Be ready to share your answers.

❶ How does Annie feel in the false passages? State the words from the text that make you think so.

❷ Use the text to tell about the setting. How do the details help you to picture the setting?

❸ What in the text shows that Jack is acting like a good big brother to Annie?

Name _____ Date _____

Mummies in the Morning

Making Connections—Writing in Code

Directions: Hieroglyphs are ancient Egyptian picture writing, where a picture represents sounds or letters in each word. In the space below, invent your own picture writing. Then, write a message. Remember to include a translation or a key!

_____

_____

© Shell Education

Mummies in the Morning

Name _____ Date _____

Language Learning–Dictionary Skills

Directions: Choose four words from the book that are new to you. Lookup each word in the dictionary. Write the part of speech and the definition for each word.

Language Hints!

Only singular words and present tense words are in the dictionary. You may have to change the ending of your word to look it up.

Word	Part of Speech	Definition

Name _____ Date _____

Mummies in the Morning

Story Elements-Plot

Directions: Jack and Annie are startled when a tomb robber runs past them and drops a scepter. Write a story that tells what happens to the tomb robber.

Mummies in the Morning

Name _____ Date _____

Story Elements–Character

Directions: Think about the relationship between Queen Hutepi and her brother. Is it like the relationship between Jack and Annie? Use the Venn diagram to compare and contrast the sets of siblings.

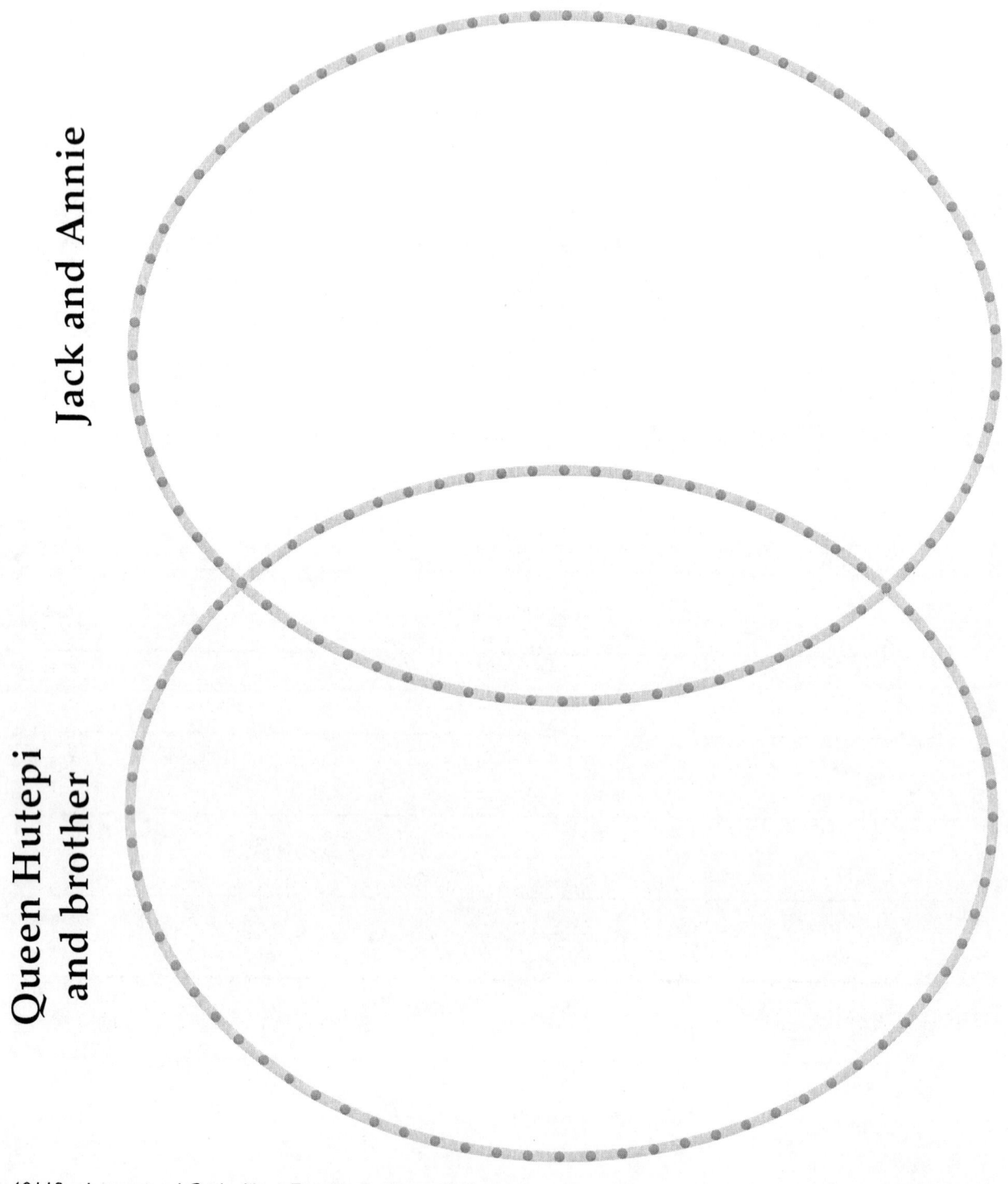

Section 4
Pirates Past Noon

Book Summary of *Pirates Past Noon*

In Frog Creek, Pennsylvania, Jack and his sister, Annie, find a magical tree house that transports them to different times and places. The tree house is filled with books that immediately capture Jack's interest in learning and Annie's love of adventure.

On a windy, rainy day, Jack and Annie return once again to the tree house they found near their house. Annie finds an open book in the corner. The picture on the page shows a warm, sunny beach. Without reading the title of the book, Annie wishes they were there. They quickly find themselves in the presence of pirates, and soon they are captured! The pirates think Jack and Annie know where the treasure is buried on the island.

Cross-Curricular Connection

Pirates Past Noon can be used in conjunction with units on maps, geography, and the history of sailing exploration.

Possible Texts for Text Sets

- Bunting, Eve. 2014. *P is for Pirate: A Pirate Alphabet*. Sleeping Bear Press.
- Havercroft, Elizabeth. 2009. *A Year on a Pirate Ship (Time Goes By)*. First Avenue Editions.
- Mizielinska, Aleksandra, and Daniel Mizielinski. 2013. *Maps*. Big Picture Press.

Section 4
Pirates Past Noon

Vocabulary Overview

Key words and phrases from this section are provided below with definitions and sentences about how the words are used in the story. Introduce and discuss these important vocabulary words with students. If you think these words or other words in the story warrant more time devoted to them, there are suggestions in the introduction for other vocabulary activities (page 5).

Word	Definition	Sentence about Text
flinging (ch. 1)	throwing or swinging with force	The wind is **flinging** rain everywhere.
parrot (ch. 1)	a brightly colored tropical bird	Annie names the **parrot** Polly.
squawk (ch. 1)	a harsh, short scream	Jack and Annie hear a **squawk** outside the tree house.
horizon (ch. 2)	the line where the earth or sea seems to meet the sky	Jack sees a ship on the **horizon**.
rowboat (ch. 3)	a small boat that is moved by rowing oars	Jack sees a **rowboat** coming closer to shore.
ragged (ch. 4)	rough or uneven	The pirate has a **ragged** beard.
lubbers (ch. 5)	unskilled seamen	The captain calls Jack and Annie **lubbers**.
pouch (ch. 5)	a small bag that can be closed	The pirate has a **pouch** at his waist.
hoist (ch. 6)	to forcefully raise	The pirates **hoist** Jack and Annie onto the ship.
cabin (ch. 6)	a small private room on a ship	Jack and Annie are locked in the captain's **cabin**.
gale (ch. 7)	a very strong wind	The pirates are afraid of the coming **gale**.
omen (ch. 8)	a sign or warning	The pirates think Polly is a bad **omen**.

Name _____ Date _____

Pirates Past Noon

Vocabulary Activity

Directions: Draw what Jack sees as he stands on the beach. Be sure to include these three words from the story.

Words from the Story

| parrot | horizon | rowboat |

Directions: Answer this question.

1. Why would the pirates fear a **gale**?

_____

_____

Section 4
Pirates Past Noon

Analyzing the Literature

Provided here are discussion questions you can use in small groups, with the whole class, or for written assignments. Each question is written at two levels so that you can choose the right question for each group of students. For each question, a few key points are provided for your reference as you discuss the book with students.

Story Element	Level 1	Level 2	Key Discussion Points
Plot	What are the pirates looking for on the island?	Why do the pirates think Jack and Annie know where the treasure is?	The pirates are looking for Captain Kidd's treasure. They find the medallion and think Jack and Annie know where the treasure is buried on the island.
Setting	What is the shape of the island?	Why is the shape of the island important?	The island is shaped like a whale. The treasure map says that the treasure is buried under the whale's eye.
Character	Who is Polly?	What is Polly trying to do?	Polly is Morgan le Fay. She is trying to help and protect Jack and Annie.
Character	After Morgan leaves, what does Jack find?	How does Morgan let Jack and Annie know that she will be coming back?	Jack finds the gold medallion in his pocket. Morgan leaves the gold medallion in Jack's pocket to let him know she will be back.

Name _____ Date _____

Pirates Past Noon

Reader Response

Think
Think about reading. What are some things you can do to be a better reader?

Informative/Explanatory Writing Prompt
Cap'n Bones cannot read. Write a list of steps he can follow to learn how to become a reader.

_____
_____
_____
_____
_____
_____
_____
_____

Pirates Past Noon

Name _____ Date _____

Guided Close Reading

Closely reread chapter 5, beginning with, "He reached into a belt pouch and pulled out a torn piece of paper." Read up to the part when Jack and Annie are tossed into the rowboat.

Directions: Think about these questions. In the space below, write ideas or draw pictures as you think. Be ready to share your answers.

❶ What do you learn about Cap'n Bones? Use the text to explain.

❷ How do Stinky and Pinky feel about Cap'n Bones? State words or phrases from the text that tell how they feel.

❸ Why does Jack agree to read the map for Cap'n Bones? Use the text to support your answer.

Name _____ Date _____

Pirates Past Noon

Making Connections–Be a Map Maker!

Directions: Maps are drawings that show a bird's-eye view of a place. Draw a map of your school, including a compass rose and a map key.

Pirates Past Noon

Name _____ Date _____

Language Learning–Idioms

Directions: Imagine if idioms only had literal meanings. Illustrate the following idioms to show their literal meanings.

Language Hints!

Idioms are phrases that have different meanings from the literal meanings of the phrases.

Example: Raining cats and dogs

fell silent

piled on the shore

the storm broke over the island

Name _____ Date _____

Pirates Past Noon

Story Elements–Plot

Directions: If Cap'n Bones goes back to the island after the storm passes, do you think he will find the treasure chest? Write a story about what he might find if he goes back.

_____
_____
_____
_____
_____
_____
_____
_____
_____
_____
_____
_____
_____
_____

Pirates Past Noon

Name _____ Date _____

Story Elements–Character

Directions: Pirate captains are always looking for people to join their crews. Pretend you are Cap'n Bones. Create an ad describing what you want in a new crew member.

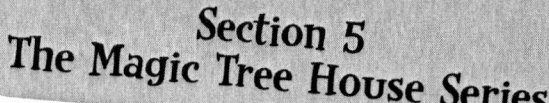

Vocabulary Overview

Directions: Choose ten words from any of the Magic Tree House books. Then, add the word and its page or chapter number to the chart. Pair students to look up the words in the dictionary and complete the chart.

Word	Definition

The Magic Tree House Series Name _____ Date _____

Vocabulary Activity

Directions: The Magic Tree House books have many vocabulary words that are specific to the settings of the stories. Draw the setting of one book. Then, label items in your picture with vocabulary words from the story.

Directions: Answer this question.

1. What is one thing that would change if this story were to have a different setting?

_____

_____

Section 5
The Magic Tree House Series

Analyzing the Literature

Provided below are discussion questions you can use in small groups, with the whole class, or for written assignments. Each question is written at two levels so that you can choose the right question for each group of students. For each question, a few key points are provided for your reference as you discuss the book with students.

Story Element	Level 1	Level 2	Key Discussion Points
Character	When Annie sees a new situation, what does she do?	Describe how Jack and Annie each have different approaches to new situations.	When Annie sees a new situation, she is excited and rushes forward with great enthusiasm. While Annie trusts her instincts, Jack prefers to research and plan before starting something new.
Character	What is Jack like at the end of the series? What is Annie like?	How have Jack and Annie changed from the beginning of the series to the end?	At the end of the series, Jack is braver and more willing to have real experiences instead of simply reading about them. Annie has learned to be a bit more careful and let Jack take care of her instead of being quick to get herself into a dangerous situation.
Plot	What is the main problem in the series?	What is the main problem and resolution in the series?	The main problem in the series is that Jack and Annie do not know to whom the tree house belongs, and they do not understand how the tree house is able to transport them to different time periods and places. In the fourth book, the kids find out that the tree house belongs to Morgan le Fay. She explains that Jack and Annie are the only people to discover her invisible magical tree house.
Setting	When and where do Annie and Jack go?	How does the setting influence the story?	The kids visit the Cretaceous period, a medieval period castle, ancient Egypt, and an island with pirates. The time and location impact the stories because of the knowledge the kids gain at each place and the courage each place inspires in them.

The Magic Tree House Series

Name _____ Date _____

Reader Response

Think

Have you ever had so much fun that you didn't want it to end? Think about a time when you wished you could stay and continue having fun.

Narrative Writing Prompt

Jack and Annie always come back to Frog Creek. Choose one Magic Tree House book. Imagine that Jack and Annie stay on their adventure a little longer. Write a new ending to that story.

_____
_____
_____
_____
_____
_____
_____
_____
_____
_____

Name _____ Date _____

The Magic Tree House Series

Guided Close Reading

Choose your favorite Magic Tree House adventure. Then, closely reread the part where Jack and Annie first land in the new setting.

Directions: Think about these questions. In the space below, write ideas or draw pictures as you think. Be ready to share your answers.

❶ What sentence in the story tells you where they land?

❷ Who is the first person to go down the ladder into the new setting? Why?

❸ Are they prepared for this new setting? Explain why or why not.

© Shell Education — 40112—Instructional Guide: Magic Tree House Series Guide — 57

The Magic Tree House Series

Name _____ Date _____

Making Connections–A Good Book . . . or a Great Book?

Directions: A book review is a mix of facts about the characters, the plot, and the setting. It shares the opinion of the author of the review. Choose a Magic Tree House book, and write a review about it. Include the following information: main characters, setting, problem, solution, and your favorite part. Also, write whether you think it is a good book to read.

_____

_____

_____

_____

_____

_____

_____

_____

_____

_____

Name _____ Date _____

The Magic Tree House Series

Language Learning–The Power of Punctuation!

Directions: Find several sentences from a Magic Tree House book that you think would be good for punctuation practice. Copy the sentences, but leave out all the punctuation. Find a partner, and exchange papers. Have your partner fill in the missing punctuation. Use your book to check your partner's answers.

Language Hints!

Punctuation includes periods, exclamation points, question marks, commas, and quotation marks. Remember to use correct capitalization, too!

1. _____

   _____

2. _____

   _____

3. _____

   _____

4. _____

   _____

The Magic Tree House Series

Name _____ Date _____

Story Elements-Plot

Directions: Choose a Magic Tree House book. Describe the problem. Then, tell how the problem is resolved. Use examples from the text to support your thinking.

Problem	Resolution

Name _____ Date _____

The Magic Tree House Series

Story Elements–Character

Directions: Choose one character, Jack or Annie. Write a list of interview questions you would like to ask the character to find out more about him or her.

_____

_____

_____

_____

_____

_____

_____

_____

_____

_____

_____

_____

_____

_____

Post-Reading Activities

Name _____ Date _____

Post-Reading Theme Thoughts

Directions: Choose Jack or Annie. Pretend you are that character. Draw a picture of a happy face or a sad face to show how the character would feel about each statement. Then, use words to explain your picture.

Character I Chose: _____

Statement	How Do You Feel? 🙂 ☹️	Explain Your Answer
Real things are always better than make-believe.		
Reading about things is better than experiencing them in real life.		
It can be fun to hang out with your little brother or sister.		
Older brothers or sisters are always braver than their younger siblings.		

Name _____ Date _____

Post-Reading Activities

Culminating Activity: Compare and Contrast

Directions: Jack and Annie have many exciting adventures. Choose two of their adventures and complete the Venn diagram. Consider how the adventure begins and ends, where they go, challenges they face, and any help they receive.

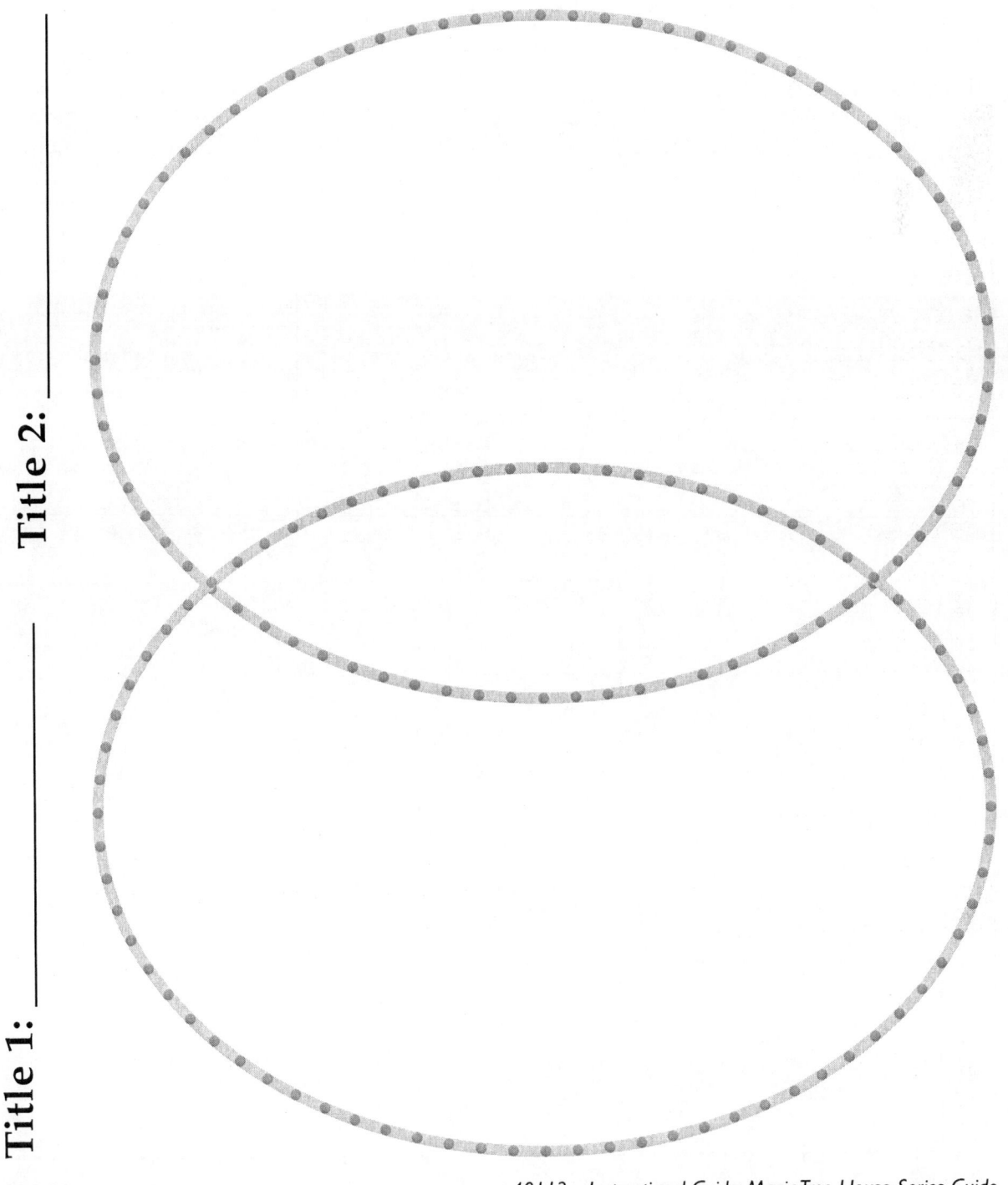

Title 2: _____

Title 1: _____

Post-Reading Activities

Name _____ Date _____

Culminating Activity: Climb the Steps!

Directions: Think about a time or a place you would like to visit or a person you would like to meet. On a separate sheet of paper, write your own Magic Tree House adventure. Consider how the adventure begins and ends, where you go, challenges you might face, people you might meet, and any help you might receive. Use the steps to help you plan your adventure. Start by choosing your setting, and then work your way down to the end of your adventure.

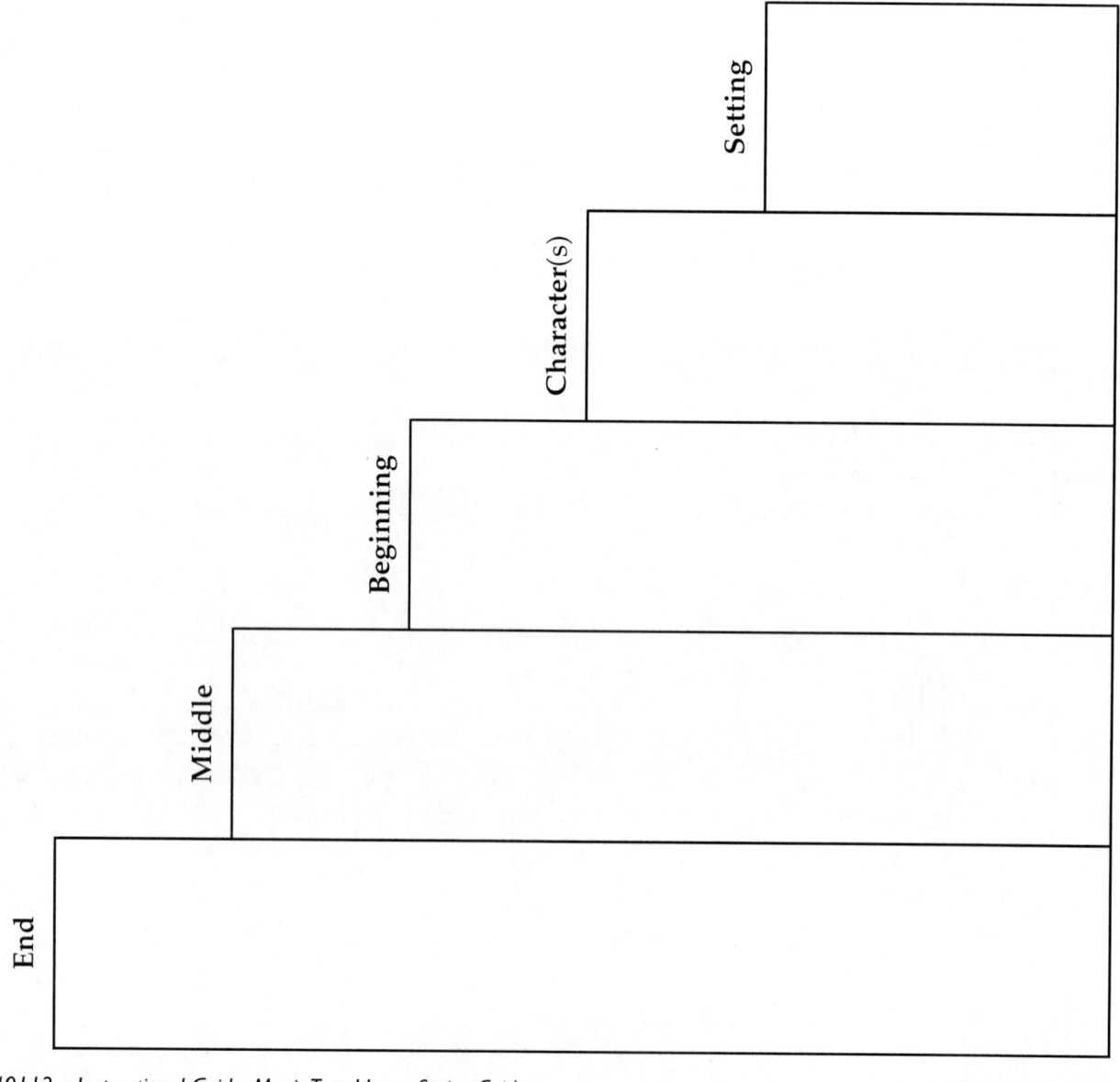

Name _____ **Date** _____

Post-Reading Activities

Comprehension Assessment

Directions: Fill in the bubble for the best response to each question.

Dinosaurs Before Dark

1. Which sentence from the book best explains why Annie was able to send the Pteranodon to rescue Jack?

    (A) "She was always trying to make friends with animals."

    (B) "She was talking to him."

    (C) "She went straight to the Pteranodon."

    (D) "Jack watched Annie hop off the ladder."

The Knight at Dawn

2. What does it show about Annie when she lets the knight lift her onto his horse?

    (E) Annie wants to be a princess rescued by a knight on a horse.

    (F) Annie is too afraid and doesn't move away from the knight.

    (G) Annie is cold and wet and wants to go back into the castle.

    (H) Annie trusts her instincts and feels the knight wants to help.

Mummies in the Morning

3. When the tree house lands in the desert, why does Annie keep mentioning mummies?

    (A) She knows Jack is afraid of mummies and is teasing him.

    (B) She knows that Jack loves mummies and will overcome his fear to see one.

    (C) She wants to see a mummy, and Jack is taking too long.

    (D) She can see a mummy in the parade in the desert.

Post-Reading Activities

Comprehension Assessment (cont.)

Pirates Past Noon

4. Which event from the story makes Cap'n Bones think that Jack and Annie know where the treasure is buried?

    (E) Cap'n Bones thinks the books in the tree house will show where the gold is buried.

    (F) Jack and Annie have a treasure map of the island.

    (G) Pinky finds the gold medallion in the tree house.

    (H) He thinks they are living on the island in the tree house.

The Magic Tree House Series

5. Describe the different ways that Jack and Annie help and support each other. Use examples from the books you have read to support your thinking.

    _____

    _____

    _____

    _____

    _____

    _____

    _____

    _____

Name _____ Date _____

Post-Reading Activities

Response to Literature: To the Rescue

Directions: In the Magic Tree House series, Jack and Annie are faced with many challenging situations. They each face these situations differently. Imagine that you need to be rescued from a situation. Which character do you think would best be able to rescue you: Jack or Annie? Choose examples from at least two Magic Tree House books to support your thinking.

_____

_____

_____

_____

_____

_____

_____

_____

_____

_____

Post-Reading Activities Name _____ Date _____

Response to Literature: The Magic Tree House Series

Directions: Answer these questions, using details from the Magic Tree House series you have read to support your thinking.

1. Choose one Magic Tree House book. Tell who made a bigger impact on the outcome of the story, Jack or Annie. Remember to support your answer with examples from the book.

   _____
   _____
   _____
   _____

2. Jack and Annie are very different. Think about a friend you have that is different from you. Is it easy to be friends? Why or why not?

   _____
   _____
   _____

3. The setting is different in each Magic Tree House book. Tell how the setting is an important part of the story.

   _____
   _____
   _____
   _____

Name _____ Date _____

Post-Reading Activities

Response to Literature Rubric

Directions: Use this rubric to evaluate student responses.

Great Job	Good Work	Keep Trying
☐ You answered all three questions completely. You included many details.	☐ You answered all three questions.	☐ You did not answer all three questions.
☐ Your handwriting is very neat. There are no spelling errors.	☐ Your handwriting can be neater. There are some spelling errors.	☐ Your handwriting is not very neat. There are many spelling errors.
☐ You used at least two examples. The examples clearly support your choice.	☐ You used at least two examples.	☐ You did not use two examples and/or the examples do not support your choice.
☐ Creativity is clear in the writing.	☐ There is creativity in the writing.	☐ There is not much creativity in the writing.

Teacher Comments: _____

_____

_____

_____

Writing Paper Name _____ Date _____

Answer Key

The responses provided here are just examples of what the students may answer. Many accurate responses are possible for the questions throughout this unit.

Vocabulary Activity—Section 1:
Dinosaurs Before Dark (page 15)
- Jack read the **caption** to learn more about the Pteranodon.
- Jack likes real things, but Annie likes **pretend** things.
- Jack could not believe they were looking at **ancient** creatures.
- Jack tries not to **panic** when he sees the Tyrannosaurus rex.
- The wind starts **whistling** as the tree house begins to spin.
1. Jack wants to **examine** the Pteranodon because he is thinking like a scientist. He wants to record his observations about the Pteranodon in his notebook.

Guided Close Reading—Section 1:
Dinosaurs Before Dark (page 18)
1. We learn that Jack likes to carefully think before doing new things, but he tells himself not to think so much.
2. amazing, miracle, felt like a bird, light as a feather, whooped, laughed
3. They teetered this way. Then that; Jack nearly fell off.

Language Learning—Section 1:
Dinosaurs Before Dark (page 20)
1. "The ⟨monster's⟩ coming!"   monster is
2. "⟨It's⟩ time to go home."   It is
3. "⟨I've⟩ never seen it before."   I have
4. "But ⟨I'm⟩ going up."   I am
5. "⟨There's⟩ our house."   There is

Vocabulary Activity—Section 2:
The Knight at Dawn (page 25)
1. Jack worries that crocodiles might be in the **moat** around the castle.

Guided Close Reading—Section 2:
The Knight at Dawn (page 28)
1. "'I want to see what's really going on, Jack. Not what's in the book,' said Annie."
2. Annie wants to experience things in real life and not just read about them. "'I want to see what's really going on, Jack. Not what's in the book,' said Annie. Jack was busy looking at the pictures in the book, instead of what was happening right in front of him. 'You can look at the book. I'm going to the real feast,' said Annie."
3. The author uses Annie's words and the captions from Jack's book to describe the setting. "'The knight's crossing the bridge,' said Annie." "'Look!' said Annie, peering through the mist. 'A windmill!'" "'Yeah, there's a windmill in here, too,' said Jack, pointing at the picture."

Vocabulary Activity—Section 3:
Mummies in the Morning (page 35)
1. Because of her poor eyesight, Jack draws a very large picture of the last part of the **hieroglyphs** in his notebook.

Guided Close Reading—Section 3:
Mummies in the Morning (page 38)
1. Annie is worried. She uses a "small voice" to answer Jack. "Annie took his hand in the dark. She squeezed it."
2. "They felt their way through the darkness." The "wooden door" "wouldn't budge." "Jack felt the stone wall as he climbed slowly down the stairs."
3. "'Don't worry. Everything's going to be okay,' said Jack. He was trying to stay calm."

Answer Key

Vocabulary Activity—Section 4:
Pirates Past Noon (page 45)
1. A **gale** could capsize a rowboat or even sink a larger ship.

Guided Close Reading—Section 4:
Pirates Past Noon (page 48)
1. The captain is a fierce man who is used to getting what he wants. "Cap'n Bones gave Jack and Annie a dark look. 'Read it,' he growled. 'Hang it! Take 'em back to the ship!' shouted Cap'n Bones. 'They can rot there till they're ready to tell us how to find Kidd's treasure!'" Cap'n Bones also has a weakness—he cannot read.
2. Stinky and Pinky feel protective of Cap'n Bones. They yell at Jack when they think he is teasing Cap'n Bones about not being able to read.
3. Jack believes that Cap'n Bones will let them go if they read the map for him. "Aye, lubber. When the treasure's in me hands, I'll let you go."

Comprehension Assessment (pages 65–66)
1. B. "She was talking to him."
2. H. Annie trusts her instincts and feels the knight wants to help.
3. B. She knows that Jack loves mummies and will overcome his fear to see one.
4. G. Pinky finds the gold medallion in the tree house.
5. Annie is always trying to make sure that Jack doesn't miss real life while he is lost in his books. Jack is always trying to make sure that Annie's spontaneous spirit does not get her into trouble.